I want to be President

I WANT TO BE
President

DAN LIEBMAN

FIREFLY BOOKS

A FIREFLY BOOK

Published by Firefly Books Ltd. 2009

First Printing

Publisher Cataloging-in-Publication Data (U.S.)
(Library of Congress Standards)

Liebman, Daniel.
    I want to be President / Dan Liebman.
[24] p. : col. photos. ; cm.   I want to be.
ISBN-13: 978-1-55407-562-1 (bound)
ISBN-10: 1-55407-562-9 (bound)
ISBN-13: 978-1-55407-563-8 (pbk.)
ISBN-10: 1-55407-563-7 (pbk.)
1. Presidents – Vocational guidance – Juvenile literature.
I. Title. II. Series.
321.8042 dc22   JF255.L54 2009

National Library of Canada Cataloguing in
Publication Data

Liebman, Daniel.
    I want to be president / Dan Liebman.
ISBN-13: 978-1-55407-562-1 (bound)
ISBN-10: 1-55407-562-9 (bound)
ISBN-13: 978-1-55407-563-8 (pbk.)
ISBN-10: 1-55407-563-7 (pbk.)
1. Student government--Juvenile literature.
2. Presidents--Juvenile literature. I. Title.
LB3092.L53 2009   j371.5'9   C2009-902352-0

Published in the United States by
Firefly Books (U.S.) Inc.
P.O. Box 1338, Ellicott Station
Buffalo, New York 14205

Published in Canada by
Firefly Books Ltd.
66 Leek Crescent
Richmond Hill, Ontario L4B 1H1

Photo Credits:

Image of the U.S. Federal Government, page 8, front cover

© George A. Walker, pages 6, 7, 9, 10, 13, 14–15, 16, 17, 18, 21, 22, back cover

© Getty Images, pages 5, 11, 19, 20, 23

© AFP / Getty Images, page 12

Acknowledgments:

The author and the publisher would like to thank Ms. Elkerton's class, Mr. Nunes' class and Mr. Scanga for their participation and ideas.

The publisher gratefully acknowledges the financial support for our publishing program by the Government of Canada through the Book Publishing Industry Development Program.

Printed in China

It isn't easy to be a president. Every president must think about many things and do many jobs. People count on their president.

How do you become a president?

Presidents are elected. A person who wants to be elected is called a candidate.

There are different kinds of presidents. This is the President of the United States.

And this boy is running for class president. He is making a speech.

This girl is telling other students why they should vote for her friend. She is campaigning.

Candidates share their ideas with voters. They explain what they will do if they are elected.

There is a lot of work to do before the election.

Each candidate has a team of helpers. These helpers are making posters.

Today is election day. It is important that everybody votes.

This student is marking a ballot. The ballot shows who she is voting for.

After the vote, the ballots are counted. The person with the most votes is the winner.

The President of the United States is being sworn in. He is making a promise to do his best for the country.

The President of the United States knows he has a big job to do. He thanks the people who helped him.

Class presidents help plan activities. They raise money. They listen to other people's ideas.

You are never too young to think about becoming a president.

HERE ARE SOME TIPS IF YOU WANT TO RUN FOR PRESIDENT:

Find out a lot about many different subjects.
Be nice.
Put up posters.
Make sure everybody hears your speech.
A speech should be interesting. It can also be funny.
Don't make other people look bad.
Don't boast if you win.
Don't make promises you can't keep.

And remember:

A president should listen to *everybody's* ideas.